overcoming
allergies

TRIDENT
REFERENCE PUBLISHING

Published by:
Trident Reference Publishing
801 12th Avenue South, Suite 400
Naples, Fl 34102 USA
Phone: + 1 239 649 7077
Email: sales@trident-international.com
Website: www.trident-international.com

Overcoming Allergies
© Trident Reference Publishing

Publisher
Simon St. John Bailey

Editor-in-chief
Isabel Toyos

Art Director
Aline Talavera

Photos
© Trident Reference Publishing, © Getty Images,
© Jupiter Images, © Planstock, © J. Alonso

Includes index
ISBN 1582799660 (hc)
UPC 615269996607 (hc)
ISBN 1582799547 (pbk)
UPC 615269995471 (pbk)

2005 Edition
Printed in USA

overcoming allergies

Rigo 8291

What are allergies?

An allergy is a catch-all word for a wide variety of reactions to substances such as pollen, cat hair, or other substances that the body determines to be foreign. Statistics state that nearly 15 percent of the current population suffers from allergies, and in some cases serious allergies.

Allergies are the result of a hypersensitive immune system. The allergic immune system misidentifies an otherwise innocuous substance as harmful, and then attacks the substance with a ferocity far greater than required. Allergic people are hypersensitive to some elements that most people find innocuous or harmless. Common allergic triggers include pollen, cigarette smoke, dust mites, feathers and animal hair or dandruff, certain foods, house dust and, in some mere cases, contact with very cold air or water can cause an allergic reaction.

THE MOST COMMON ALLERGIES

Some of the most common allergic reactions include:
• **Seasonal sinus allergies.** This allergy, also known as "hay fever", is the most common. Symptoms include: sneezing, runny nose, nasal congestion, itchy, watery eyes and itchy mouth, ears and throat. Exposure to pollen and dust mites can trigger hay fever or seasonal allergies. Dust mites are microscopic organisms that live in house dust, a mixture of potentially allergenic materials including fibers from different fabrics, dandruff from animals, bacteria, mold or fungus spores.
• **Asthma.** Though asthma is not always triggered by

allergies, it is related to them. Most adults with asthma have an allergy-related condition. During an asthma attack the lining of the airways becomes swollen or inflamed and the cells that line the airways produce more mucus, which is thicker than normal. Symptoms include frequent cough, shortness of breath, wheezing and chest tightness, pain, or pressure.

• **Food allergies.** The body often reacts to foods, although only a small amount of those reactions are true allergies that are involved with the immune system. The most common allergies are to foods including milk, chocolate, eggs, fish, shellfish, wheat, soy, peanuts and other types of nut.

• **Skin allergies.** Atopic eczema and allergic contact dermatitis occur in people who are allergic to a specific ingredient or ingredients in a product. Symptoms include inflammation, redness, swelling, itching, and hive-like breakouts.

• **Allergic reactions to insect stings.** Bee, wasp, yellow jacket, hornet or fire ant stings most often trigger allergic reactions. Symptoms of a severe allergic reaction, called an "anaphylactic reaction", may include: difficulty breathing, hives that appear as a red, itchy rash and spread to areas beyond the sting, swelling of the face, throat or mouth tissue, wheezing or difficulty swallowing, in extreme cases putting the sufferer at risk of death.

LIFE AT RISK

Anaphylaxis is the word used for a serious and rapid allergic reaction usually involving more than one part of the body which, if severe enough, can kill. When exposed to a severe allergen the sufferer may have a severe allergic response, also known as anaphylaxis. In the case of anaphylaxis it's necessary to get immediate, emergency medical attention for an adrenaline or cortisone shot. If the severe allergic response is caused by an insect bite, do not touch the affected area, because it can cause the venom further penetrate to the skin.

FACTS ABOUT ALLERGIES

• One in every three people has suffered from allergies at some point in their lives.

• Hay fever or seasonal allergy affects one in five people.

• One in every five school children suffers from asthma, the most common causes are allergies.

• One in every six children suffers from skin problems, in particular eczema, associated with some allergies.

• One in every twenty people suffers from some type of skin eruption such as hives.

• Food allergies are often worse, but fortunately they aren't frequent.

• Allergic reactions from insect bites or bee stings affect ten percent of the population.

What can trigger allergies?

There are a number of different allergy-causing substances a person might react to, depending on their genetics. These are some of the most frequent allergens, allergy diagnosis and treatments.

• **Dust mites.** They are microscopic organisms that live in house dust. House dust is a mixture of potentially allergenic materials including fibers from different fabrics, dandruff from animals, bacteria, mold or fungus spores, food particles, bits of plants, dead skin and other things. Dust mites accumulate in carpets, mattresses and pillows. Their defecations cause allergic reactions in hypersensitive skin. This trigger affects 90 percent of people who suffer from allergies.

• **The pollen of flowers and tree blossom.** Provokes reactions in 70 percent of allergic people.

• **Domestic animals.** They are the third most common cause of allergic reaction; 40 percent of asthmatic children have allergic reactions to the proteins secreted by the oil glands in an animal's skin, as well as to the proteins present in an animal's saliva or urine.

• **Molds.** They are microscopic fungi with spores that float in the air like pollen. In the fall molds are more common. They can bring on sever asthma attacks.

• **Foods.** In this allergy trigger group, the most common allergic foods are milk, chocolate, eggs, fish and peanuts. Colorants and preservatives can also trigger allergic reactions.

• **Medications.** Some people develop allergies to certain medications. The best treatment of drug allergies is to avoid the offending drug altogether. There are a number of ingredients in cosmetics and perfumes that can trigger allergies in some people.

DIAGNOSIS AND TREATMENT

An important part of diagnosing allergies is a careful evaluation of your symptoms. Your doctor will ask you several questions to rule out other conditions that may cause allergy-like symptoms. You should inform your doctor about the environmental conditions around you (home, work, contact with animals), triggering factors that provoke symptoms, family history with allergies, etc. Other tests may be performed –based on your doctor's recommendations after the medical history and examination– to determine which allergens are causing your symptoms. These may include a skin test or a blood test. In both, a sample is taken from the allergy sufferer and analyzed for antibodies. On the basis of both tests (doctors may not always be able to determine the exact cause) your physician will diagnose a specific treatment.

ENVIRONMENTAL POLLUTION

In the past 100 years allergies and cases of asthma have increased significantly, especially in children and young adults. There is evidence that air pollutants worsen allergies and asthma. High concentrates of nitrogen dioxide (NO_2) and a large array of particles in the air, due to a high emission of diesel exhaust, are significant factors in air pollution spurring allergies.

SMOKING BANNED

Cigarette smoke contains a number of toxic chemicals and irritants. People with allergies may be more sensitive to cigarette smoke than other people, and research studies indicate that smoking may aggravate allergies. Smoking does not just harm smokers but also those around them. Research has shown that children and spouses of smokers tend to have more respiratory infections and asthma than those of non-smokers. In addition, exposure to secondhand smoke can increase the risk of complications such as sinusitis and bronchitis. Not only cigarette smoke is irritating, smoke from wood stoves and chimneys can also be irritating for asthmatics. They release certain chemicals including sulfur dioxide. If you can, avoid wood stoves and fireplaces, and keep the room well ventilated.

Anti-allergenic house

Our homes are our sanctuary for getting away from every day tension. However, they aren't always allergy free. A number of allergens can be found in our homes. Here are some general rules for avoiding allergic triggers in your home that can be bothersome for some family members.

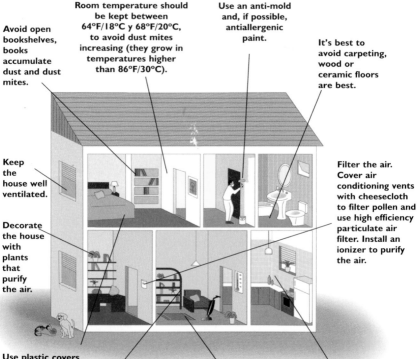

Avoid open bookshelves, books accumulate dust and dust mites.

Room temperature should be kept between 64°F/18°C y 68°F/20°C, to avoid dust mites increasing (they grow in temperatures higher than 86°F/30°C).

Use an anti-mold and, if possible, antiallergenic paint.

It's best to avoid carpeting, wood or ceramic floors are best.

Keep the house well ventilated.

Decorate the house with plants that purify the air.

Filter the air. Cover air conditioning vents with cheesecloth to filter pollen and use high efficiency particulate air filter. Install an ionizer to purify the air.

Use plastic covers for pillows, mattresses and box springs. Avoid overstuffed furniture and down-filled bedding or pillows. Wash your bedding every week in hot water at 158°F/70°C, to eliminate microorganisms.

Avoid overstuffed furniture that accumulates dust.

Avoid dust-collecting Venetian blinds or long drapes. Replace old drapes with window shades instead. Limit throw rugs to reduce dust and mold. If you do have rugs, make sure they are washable.

Avoid using brooms or feathered dusters. Use a damp cloth to clean dust. Avoid insecticides, products with ammonia and aerosols.

The air we breathe carries a lot of different micro particles of different sizes. Some originate in the home and others enter the home through windows, doors and heating systems. For most people micro particles floating in the air do not cause any problems. But for those who suffer from allergic symptoms –including asthma– the allergic triggers may be found in their own homes. Take a number of precautions to help prevent allergies:

■ Reduce or get rid of any factor that triggers asthma and allergies.

■ Use filters and air conditioners to keep the house cleaner and more comfortable.

■ Try to prevent or get rid of dust mites, especially in the bedroom.

■ Limit fans and vacuum cleaners, because they can stir up dust and a number of allergens found in the air. A fan with an air filter can relatively be an alternative solution. If that doesn't work, cover air conditioning vents with cheesecloth to filter pollen and use a high efficiency particulate air filter.

OTHER FACTORS

- **Smoke.** Don't allow smoking in your house. Avoid wood stoves and fireplaces.
- **Animals.** If you have pets, consider keeping them outside or perhaps ask someone else to take care of them. If you must keep your pets indoors, do not allow them in the bedroom and be sure to bathe them often.
- **Mold.** When there is a high level of humidity, mold can be a problem, especially in the bathroom, kitchen and basement. It's best to keep these places well ventilated and clean. Install dehumidifiers in basement and other areas of the house where molds tend to collect. Clean these devices every week. Don't collect too many indoor plants as soil encourages mold growth.
- **Perfumes or strong fumes.** Perfume, air sprays and chemical cleaning products, paint and talc can be allergy triggers and should be avoided. Limit exposure to chemicals.

Prevention is best...

The key in treating any allergy is preventing exposure to the trigger allergen. Since this isn't always possible, there are a number of other ways to reduce symptoms for some cases, such as hay fever and insect bites.

SEASONAL HAY FEVER

Hay fever, also known as "seasonal allergic rhinitis" is an allergic response to pollen (the male component of the plant reproductive system) or other microscopic substances that are present only at certain times of the year. Allergic rhinitis can also be perennial (year-round). Sneezing, runny nose, and itchy, watery eyes accompany seasonal attacks (spring or summer). Hay fever affects 10 percent to 20 percent of the world population. It's impossible to eliminate pollen floating in the air, however, there are a number of precautions you can take to limit exposure to this allergen:

- In the spring and summer, if possible, stay indoors early in the afternoon, when outdoor pollen counts are usually highest.
- If possible, sleep with the window closed to prevent pollen from entering the room.

DIAGNOSING

People who react to a bee sting or insect bite with a hive or swelling in more than 4 in/10 cm of the skin, or have a general reaction with itchiness, asthma or a drop in blood pressure, should visit their doctor for a RAST blood test or skin scratch test, to diagnose allergies to insect bites. Allergy specialists can then consider what is the necessary treatment.

- Use sunglasses, to impede contact between pollen and the eyes.
- Don't cut the grass yourself and avoid being around freshly cut grass if possible.
- Keep windows closed and set the air conditioner to use re-circulated air if you are allergic to pollen.
- When choosing a vacation spot, think about going to the beach, because coastal areas tend to have lower pollen count.

BEE STINGS OR INSECT BITES

Bee, wasp, yellow jacket, hornet or fire ant stings most often trigger allergic reactions. Wasps generally bite in the summer and fall, during winter only the queen survives. Bees are less aggressive but their venom penetrates further into the skin. Although these types of insect bites are common, only 10 percent of the population has mild allergic reactions and less than 0.5 percent has severe allergic reactions to insect venom. Here are a few tips to avoid insect bites:

- Don't make sudden moves if there are wasps or bees close by.
- Use gloves when gardening or picking fruit.
- Stay away from fruit trees and fallen fruit.
- Outdoors, don't use baggy clothing or bright colors, because they attract insects.
- Don't use perfume.
- Avoid eating outdoors.
- Don't walk barefoot.

PAY ATTENTION TO TIMES AND WEATHER
During summer and spring, in the early morning and in the evenings, outdoor pollen levels are usually highest. When the earth cools down, the pollen falls in clouds. During a storm, allergens found in the air increase considerably, because humidity makes pollen grains explode. Check the forecast. Stay indoors as much as possible on hot, dry, windy days when pollen counts are highest.

Exercises, yes or no?

For decades physical exercise and sports were discouraged for allergy and asthma sufferers, especially among children and young adults. Exercise, is an important activity for everyone, including patients who have asthma or other allergic disorders. It will help them to feel their best, both physically and psychologically.

For many people, vigorous exercise can trigger bronchial spasms and a tight chest. Working out can also cause different symptoms such as accelerated heart rate, coughing, stomach pains and chest pains that occur five to ten minutes after beginning physical exercise. This happens especially when you exercise outdoors in cold, dry weather, important factors that can worsen symptoms because the respiratory system loses heat. Air pollutants (sulfur dioxide), high pollen concentrates and viral infections in the respiratory system can increase the probability and severity of attacks induced by exercise.

BENEFICIAL SPORTS

Swimming is considered the best sport for allergy and asthma suffers. Swimming involves breathing warm and moist air and is often well tolerated. You can do this exercise all year round. In fact, it builds up the lung capacity and muscle tone of the diaphragm, much like breathing exercises. Swimming, due to the warm, humid environment, the toning of the upper body muscles, and the horizontal position (which may actually loosen mucus from the bottom of the lungs), can be very beneficial. Other recommended activities include sports that use short spurts of exertion or less vigorous exercises such as baseball, karate, wrestling, long distance running, short distance running, golf, walking, jogging and low impact aerobics.

SPORTS YOU SHOULD AVOID

Cold-weather activities, such as skiing and ice hockey, often trigger an attack or continuous vigorous exercises (basketball, field hockey, tennis or soccer) are more likely to induce bronchial spasms.

OTHER USEFUL TIPS

• Make sure you're properly warmed up. Five to ten minutes of stretching or light exercise can help relax and open up your airways.

• Exercise only when you're free of any viral respiratory infections, such as a cold. Avoid exercising when pollen or air pollution levels are high or in cold weather.

• If inhaling air through the mouth, keep the mouth pursed (lips forming a small "O" close together), so that the air is less cold and dry when it enters the airways during exercise.

Emotional balance

Beyond physical allergen factors that trigger a crisis, it's known that emotional tension can also play a factor in triggering an allergic reaction. Breathing, relaxation, visualization and meditation techniques can be beneficial exercises for preventing and relieving symptoms.

✛ Learning how to relax is fundamental to treating allergies. And a key to relaxation is proper breathing techniques. There are three basic types of breathing: abdominal and diaphragmatic breathing; thoracic breathing; and clavicular or collarbone breathing. Complete breathing unites the three techniques and increases lung capacity. This is why these exercises are specifically recommended for allergy sufferers. They also help your overall well-being and increase the strenght of your immune system.

BREATHING
■ **Abdominal or diaphragmatic breathing**

Lie down on the floor with your hands on your abdomen. Take a deep breath, inhaling slowly through your nose and send the air to the bottom of your lungs, expanding your abdomen, concentrating your energy in that area. Hold your breath for a few seconds. Then slowly exhale, contracting your abdomen.

■ Thoracic breathing

In the same position, place your hands over the thorax and concentrate on the energy in this area. Without moving your abdomen, take a deep breath and note how your ribs rise and your chest expands as the air enters.

■ Clavicular or collarbone breathing

Using the same position, place your hands on your upper chest or on the collarbone. Inhale and exhale through the nose, paying attention to how it feels when the air lifts your ribs, collarbone and shoulders. (The body does not take in sufficient oxygen with this type of breathing, so it's best not to practice this exercise for very long.)

■ Complete breathing

Complete breathing is a combination of abdominal breathing, thoracic breathing and clavicular breathing.

First, inhale and bring the air to the bottom of your lungs, then to your thorax and finally to your upper chest. Exhale in the same order, letting the air out of the bottom of your lungs, thorax and finally the upper chest.

SITALI BREATHING

This exercise is very beneficial for calming agitated emotional states, in particular anxiety which is so typical of the diagnostic picture shown by the person who is prone to allergies. *Sitali* breathing also purifies the blood and promotes relaxation and a general state of well-being. Put out your tongue in such a way that it protrudes just a little beyond your lips. Fold the tongue around so that it makes a "tube" and inhale as deeply as you can through this. You'll notice that the passage of air produces a whistling sound and cools the tongue. Hold the breath in each time, for as long as is comfortable, then exhale through the nose.

POWER OF THE IMAGINATION

Creative visualization uses the imagination to create situations and ideal conditions for the mind. Conscious and continuos practice of visualization helps to establish clear connections between dreams and desires. This helps to relax the mind and physical condition, providing relief of physical allergic reaction symptoms such as difficulty breathing, itchiness or sneezing. In addition to visualizing a beautiful and calm place, you can also imagine and create your desired health. Visualizing the entire respiratory process and each one of the organs functioning in complete harmony. The same visualization can work for skin allergies such as eczema. Scientific studies have shown that these types of creative visualization techniques fortify the immune system.

MEDITATION

This technique is recommended for reaching internal harmony. These are a number of the benefits of meditation:
- Helps to reduce the flow of negative thoughts and emotions.
- Reduces your anxiety and stress level.
- Increases self-actualization to explore your inner feelings and states.
- Deepens a connection with the realm of the spiritual.
- Regular practice (requires a meditation guide at the beginning) can contribute to an

individual's psychological and physiological well-being. The practice can reduce blood pressure and relieve pain and stress.

A RELAXING ENVIRONMENT

It's important to do breathing, visualization and meditation techniques in a relaxing environment.

- **Peace.** Make sure that you won't have any interruptions. If you need to, put a "Do not disturb sign" on your door.
- **Temperature.** The room should be warm, not too hot or too cold. You should avoid drafts.
- **Lighting.** Lighting should be soft. Use candles or a blue or green lamp.
- **Clothing.** Your clothes should be made of comfortable, loose and soft material.
- **Environment.** Make the environment even more comfortable by burning

incense stick or adding a few drops of an essential oil to a clay aromatherapy pot.
- **Music.** You can put on soft music or sounds from nature (flowing water, birds chirping or wind blowing) in the background to help clear your mind and bring harmony.

DEEP RELAXATION

After practicing breathing exercises lie on your back, with the palms of your hands toward the ceiling and your legs slightly spread.

Relax each part of your body, from the lower part of your body upward: feet, legs, buttocks, pelvis, back, chest, arms, shoulders, neck and your face. Each time you exhale, imagine that you are releasing your tension. Mentally repeat, "I am relaxing"... Try to concentrate on your breathing. If your thoughts interrupt you from relaxing, imagine that your thoughts float over you like a cloud when you exhale.

Yoga, a moving philosophy

Calming the nervous system, relaxing body and mind and harmonizing emotional states are the three fundamental conditions needed to help prevent and relieve allergic reactions. Yoga helps us to attain these three objectives through the practice of certain postures or *asanas*.

The practice of yoga exercises (in *Sanskrit*) means practicing your body, spirit and your mind together. With yoga postures or *asanas*, the complete breathing and relaxation techniques of this ancient art becomes a powerful defense against allergies. The following *asanas* are recommended for allergic reactions.

THE FISH

This posture is highly beneficial for your body: it regulates thyroid and pineal gland functions and helps expand the ribcage fully, which is why its recommended for cases of asthma, sinus troubles and hay fever. It also relieves the stiffness of your neck and shoulder muscles and stretches your abdominals.

1. Sit on your heels, with your back straight, looking forward and with your hands on your thighs.

2. Breathing freely, bring your head all the way back, as you arch your spine. Rest your weight on your elbows and the palms of your hands.

3. Drop your head back so that the top of your head is on the floor. You should feel how your vertebrae press together and the area around your throat opens. When you are firmly placed in this position, bring your hands to your chest and place the palms of your hands together. Stay in this position for as long as you find comfortable. To come out of the pose, place your elbows on the floor, inhale, bring your chin to your chest and roll onto your side while you exhale.

LYING DOWN SPINAL TWIST

Other than stretching the legs and toning the spinal nerves, performing this pose also expands the ribcage fully, increases your lung capacity and aids in deep breathing when you have allergic attacks.

1. Lie on your back, your body straight, your legs stretched and your arms at your sides. Lift up your right leg and bring it to your chest, supporting it with your hands on your knee. Keep your leg like this for a few seconds and then repeat with your left leg.

2. Return to the initial position. Extend your left arm out at shoulder height. Inhale, and as you exhale bend your right leg and cross it over your stretched out left leg. Try to avoid lifting your right shoulder up from the floor. Stay in this position for a few minutes, while you concentrate on your breathing. Release and repeat on the other side.

1. *From a lying position, with your arms extended next to your body, inhale and lift your legs until they form a 90 degree angle. Exhale, and when you inhale again lift up your hips and back, bringing your legs over your head.*

THE CANDLE

This posture is recommended to help treat problems with asthma and bronchitis. It regulates the function of the thyroid glands and improves overall blood circulation.

3. *Bring your right leg up, with your toes pointed to the ceiling and remain in this position as long as you can. Next, slowly lower your torso, bending your legs and placing each segment of your backbone against the floor.*

2. *Bend your arms, keep your hands back and bring your feet to the floor. Raise your left leg, streched (your chin needs to be pressed against your chest, so that your neck doesn't tense up).*

PAY ATTENTION TO BREATHING
Achieving conscious breathing is one of the fundamental requisites of yoga technique. Without proper breathing you can't relax or concentrate, the conditions needed for practicing yoga poses.

THE PLOW

This pose helps to keep your back loose, to avoid spinal tension and stretch the sciatic nerve. Practicing this pose also improves blood circulation and fortifies the immune system; this is why it's recommended for allergic patients.

GENTLE EXERCISE
Yoga is a discipline designed to improve your flexibility and your mental and emotional harmony. The exercises use gentle movements without straining the body. When practicing the *asanas* remember not to strain yourself. There is no need to push yourself too far. Remember to use gentle movements and don't push your body into a pose. Through time and willpower, you will improve your physical health naturally and get in tune with your body and mind. It is important to remember to use your body with moderation, patience and consistency to prevent side effects like sore muscles or tiredness.

1. *Begin the position lying on your back, with your legs together, arms down by your sides next to your body and palm of your hands pressed to the floor. Bring your chin toward your chest and press your back muscles to the floor. Inhale through your nose and exhale while you lift up both legs, until they are at a 90 degree angle with your torso. Exhale, then inhale and bring your hips off the floor, supporting your back with your hands.*

2. *Without bending your knees, stretch out your legs by bringing them behind your head, until your toes touch the floor. Your arms should stay forward, with the palms of your hands pressed to the floor. Stay in this position breathing slowly and deeply. Next, inhale through your nose and slowly lower your legs while you exhale. Concentrate on how each segment of your backbone presses against the floor as you come down.*

Healthy energy

Reiki is a natural healing art for personal growth using the hands. This ancient technique is not only beneficial for physical health but also emotional and mental well-being. It may help to relieve the anxiety and tension brought on by an allergic reaction.

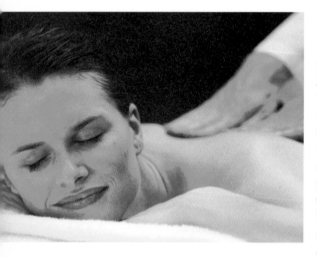

✚ The syllables *rei* and *ki* come from Japan, meaning "universal energy". *Reiki* is a healing art using the hands to transmit natural energy to the patient. Practicing *reiki* may be beneficial in relieving physical discomforts. It's a therapeutic discipline that treats the body holistically, or as one entity, including the physical body, emotions, mind and spirit, in such a way that it doesn't only remove a pathology but tries to harmonize the body's natural balance to bring well-being and happiness.

The Chakras

Reiki is also defined as light-energy that penetrates the body through seven principal *chakras*, running from the base of the spine to the top of the head.
They are:

Sahasrara. Corresponds to the *chakra* of the crown, and to the pineal gland. It is the center of union between the spirit and the physical life.

Ajna. *Chakra* at the center of the head or the "third eye." Corresponds to the pituitary gland. This is the center of morality, ethics, intuition and will power.

Vishuddha. This is the *chakra* of the throat and thyroid glands. It is related to communication and internal development; it is the point that joins the inner and external being.

Anaha. Corresponds to the heart and the thymus gland. This point represents vulnerability, dreams, love, hopes, self-esteem and spiritual life.

Manipura. This is the *chakra* of the solar plexus. It is related to the stomach, liver and digestive systems. It refers to the intellect, wisdom, and decision making.

Svadisthana. This is the point of the genital organs. It is the center for sexual energy, fertility, emotions and sensations.

Muladahra. This *chakra* corresponds to the corticoadrenal glands. It is related with basic survival, instinct, vitality and abundance.

PRINCIPLES OF REIKI

This thousand year old technique was rediscovered or researched in the 18th century by Japanese doctor Milkao Usui, who meditated on and synthesized the five principles of *reiki*, especially for the well-being of all humans:

- Just for today I will not be angry.
- Just for today I will not worry.
- Earn your living honestly.
- Honor your parents, teachers and elders.
- Show gratitude to every living thing.

Reiki, the universal curative energy is within everyone's reach. You don't need previous study to practice, you only need to be open to feeling, giving and receiving energy flow. We've provided a fourteen step routine to energize and relax, ideal for allergic patients:

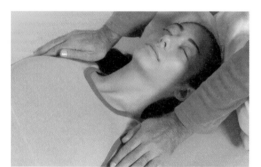

1. To reestablish the harmony in the body's energetic circulation that is easily lost during an allergic reaction, place both hands on the sides of the shoulders.

2. To relieve or overcome problems related to vocal chords or problems of communication, place the palms of the hands on the throat.

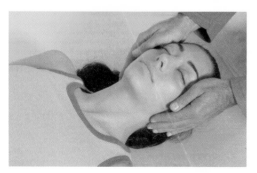

3. Most nerve ends are found in the head. Place the hands around the head, covering the ears to achieve total well-being in the body.

4. Place the hands on the temples of the patient to balance the two hemispheres and transmit healing and harmonious energy.

5. Place the hands over the forehead and eyes; this evokes the third eye and treats problems related with the eyes, sight and feelings.

6. Place the hands on the crown of the head to relieve and prevent chronic headaches and migraines.

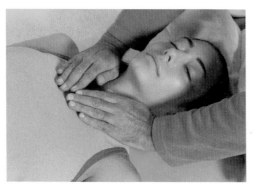

7. Place the hands on the hollow part of the chest, this emits energy to the thyroids. After, bring the hands over the heart and keep in this position for a few seconds.

8. *First, on the sides and then under the shoulders. Directing the energy over these two areas is a way to awaken the body's balance and to relieve specific pains.*

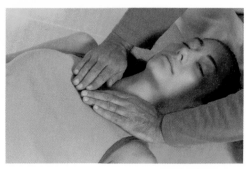

9. *Place the hands over the chest to help the function of the lungs. Rub the hands inward and outward to release negative energy.*

10. *With the palms faced upward, place the hands under the neck and work the area at the back of the neck to relax the spine and stimulate the function of the spinal cord.*

11. *Keep the hands over the abdomen; next, bring the hands to the solar plexus. This step is great for recovering energy and strengthening the body.*

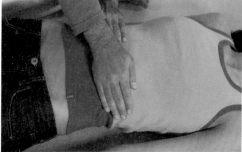

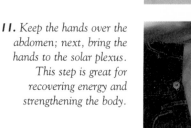

THE BENEFITS OF REIKI

- Helps to release blocked emotions.
- Has purifying effects on the body (to eliminate toxins) and on the mind (releases recurring and negative thoughts.)
- Restores harmony through balancing the *chakras,* or energy centers.
- Strengthens the immune system, activating natural defenses.
- Contributes to the awareness and development of the spirit.

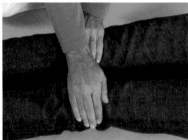

12. This is the place called the secret chakra that improves the function of the intestines and liver. This step is important to help the functioning of the ovaries and the prostate gland.

13. Continue along the knees, leaving the hands over the knees for a few minutes. This technique is recommended for relieving pains in the legs and for those who suffer from rheumatoid arthritis.

ESSENTIAL FOR REIKI

The essence of *reiki* is the energy of love. This is why giving or receiving *reiki* opens healing energy. This discipline has been defined as energy as large as radio waves, because it can be applied with direct contact or from afar. It is a harmless energy, without side effects. This is an effective complementary therapy. The skill of healing through *reiki* can only be received through a teacher; you don't need any previous knowledge, but you need to be open to giving or receiving the energy.

14. Lastly, place the hands around the ankles. This position helps relieve pains in the feet and legs, and swelling or fluid retention in the ankles.

The power of water

Water is one of the most powerful curing sources in nature, with therapeutic and preventative properties. Using hydrotherapy techniques is simple and inexpensive. This therapy is beneficial for a number of discomforts, including the skin and respiratory problems caused by allergies.

Curing techniques with water to prevent and relieve health problems has been used since ancient times. Hypocrates used hydrotherapy 2,300 years ago to cure ill patients. The following techniques

described were developed specifically to treat
skin problems and symptoms related to allergies.

CLAY WATER TO TREAT SKIN PROBLEMS

Using cold bandages improves circulation,
increasing the flow of blood to the affected area
of the body, promoting the reduction of waste
through the skin and giving a pleasant, calming
sensation. For eczema, irritated or inflamed skin
or rashes, apply cold compresses with mineral
rich clay to give immediate relief and to soften
the skin. Mix 3 tablespoons of clay with water
until it has a firm
consistency.
Refrigerate, then
place a layer
5 millimiters thick
over the skin and
cover with a towel
soaked in clay.
Change the
bandage every 10
minutes. Before
using this treatment
it's recommended
consulting your allergist.
Warning. Not recommended for people
who suffer from high blood pressure.

> **WARNING**
> Before using clay
> treatments
> consult your
> doctor.

NASAL BATHS

To contribute to a good cleaning of
the nostrils and to relieve excess
mucus, it's recommended washing both nostrils
twice daily with sea salt diluted in lukewarm
water. You can find sea salt in health food
stores and vitamin dealers.

HEALTHY STEAM

Steam baths are a great therapy for detoxifying the body. Because the treatment makes you sweat, it helps your body to expel waste while at the same time relaxing and bringing well-being to your mind and body. Steam is an effective treatment to help relieve the symptoms related to respiratory problems. Recommended treatments:

• **Finnish bath**, consists of sitting in a chamber with steam formed by pouring water with eucalyptus essence over porous, hot rocks. This steam bath is done in a closed room with temperatures up to 113 °F/45 °C. It helps to relax and relieve tensions, while at the same time the aroma released from the eucalyptus essential oil has a stimulating effect and helps the respiratory system recover. Before using this therapy for the first time, consult a medical specialist.

• **Turkish bath**, traditionally practiced in Turkey. It consists of a series of steam chambers with different temperatures ranging from 113 to 158 °F/45 to 70 °C. Heat is

PRECAUTION
It's not recommended to take steam baths if you have serious infections, low blood pressure, kidney disorder, hyper-thyroids, or clogged or clotted blood circulation (varicose veins, clogged arteries). Everyone should consult his doctor before using this therapy.

generated by hot water that circulates through pipes and radiators located along the walls of the chambers. Because of the humidity in the room, your sweat doesn't evaporate, your body can't cool down and you sweat even more.

AT HOME

▮ Facial steam with salt.
Traditionally a remedy from grandma's days, an old fashioned and sure fire way to provide relief for respiratory ailments such as hay fever and asthma: place water in a pot and add a hand full of rock salt. Allow to boil, take off the heat and add to a bowl. Breathe the steam for at least 10 minutes.

▮ To prevent congestion.
Steam from a vaporizer, when adding a few drops of essential oils, helps to keep the air humid relieving congestion.

Reflexes and well-being

Foot reflexology is a massage technique based on ancient Oriental medicine. Today, this therapy is widely known as a complementary treatment, used in clinics and hospitals throughout the world. This curative technique may be efficient in treating allergies and asthma.

✚ Reflexology is a healing technique based on the concept that on the feet there are a number of points that reflect the organs, body systems and vital functions. The different points on the feet correspond to different parts of the body. When these are stimulated, healing energy is released. That may help to improve your overall physical well-being. This treatment can be used as a complementary therapy for certain illnesses including allergies and asthma. Manipulating and pressing with firm pressure on the reflexology points, helps to relieve some allergic symptoms. After each session the patient should feel pleasantly and deeply rested.

KEY POINTS FOR EVERY DISCOMFORT

To relieve allergic reactions with reflexology, you should first massage the entire foot and then each one of the reflexology zones, in order to relax the entire body (see diagrams). Next,

apply pressure and massage to each of the
points that corresponds to the type of allergic
symptom you suffer from.

ASTHMA ATTACK

To relieve the
principal symptoms
of muscular spasms
in the bronchial
tubes, and
excessive secretion
of mucus that
obstructs the
respiratory tract,
apply gentle but
steady pressure on
the points that
correspond to the
thorax, lungs,
suprarenal glands
and solar plexus.

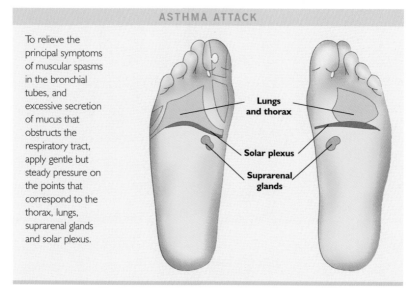

Lungs
and thorax

Solar plexus

Suprarenal
glands

SEASONAL HAY FEVER

This ailment affects
the mucous glands in
the respiratory tract
and the conjunctiva
in the eyes. Other
organs involved in
this allergic reaction
include
the large intestine,
small intestine,
thorax and lungs.

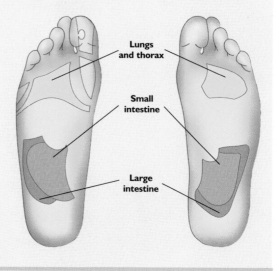

Lungs
and thorax

Small
intestine

Large
intestine

SKIN ERUPTIONS

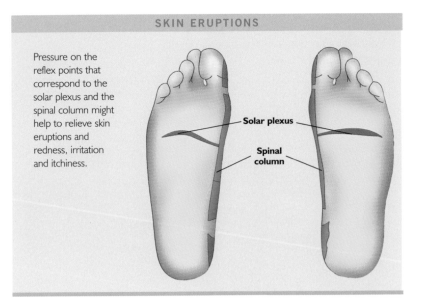

Pressure on the reflex points that correspond to the solar plexus and the spinal column might help to relieve skin eruptions and redness, irritation and itchiness.

Solar plexus

Spinal column

RELIEVING MASSAGE

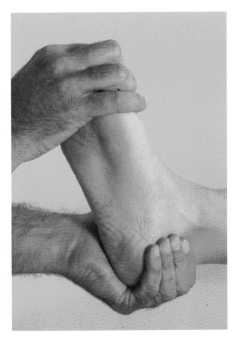

1. After washing the feet, begin by massaging the sole of each foot up to the ankle. Take the foot in your hand and roll the ankle to relieve tension. Next, massage each of the toes one by one and continue on the sole of the foot.

BENEFICIAL EFFECTS
Reflexology normalizes the body's functioning and improves blood circulation. It helps oxygen flow throughout the whole organism. Reflexology regulates the nervous system and eliminates toxins.

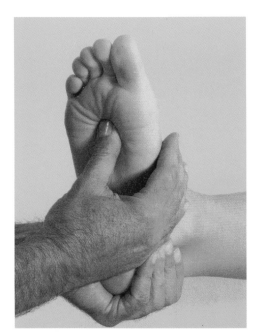

2. *Press on the reflex point that corresponds to the solar plexus to balance and harmonize the body and to relieve tensions and general stress caused by an allergic reaction. Use gentle, circular movements for a minute or two, relaxing the solar plexus. This facilitates deep breathing, rather than shallow breathing from the top part of the lungs.*

PRECAUTIONS

It's not recommended practicing reflexology on people who are suffering from fever or serious illnesses; who need surgery; who have disorders or inflammation in the lymphatic or vascular systems; when the feet are infected with fungus or more serious foot infections such as gangrene; when the subject is pregnant.

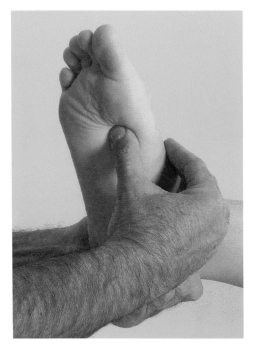

3. *Apply pressure for a few minutes on the point that corresponds to the bronchial area. Next, use circular massages for a minute. This exercise may be effective for cases of asthma, inflamed bronchial tubes and to relieve smoker's cough.*

Healthy aromas

Aromatherapy is the practice of therapeutically using pure aromas, as a natural treatment for a number of disorders, among them allergies. This treatment is a good complementary therapy to help to reestablish physical and psychological balance and harmony. Listed below are a number of tips for using natural essences correctly in allergy treatment.

Aromatherapy is a holistic discipline that uses essential oils naturally extracted from plants for their therapeutic effects. Many studies have revealed that the sense of smell is the deepest physical sense that we have which has a powerful influence over our bodies and emotions.

For treating allergies, using essential oils can bring a number of excellent benefits. From the emotional point of view, they help to relieve the tensions and anxiety brought on by allergic reactions. Using aromatherapy may help to prevent tension. From a physical point of view, beyond helping to relieve certain symptoms, aromatherapy stimulates the immune system, increasing the body's defense mechanisms.

It's important to be aware that only pure, natural, non-imitated essential oils have medicinal properties for effective treatment.

Perfumes, shampoos and bath lotions with herbs, although they have a pleasant aroma, don't have therapeutic actions.

MODES OF USE

■ **Vaporizers.** This is another effective treatment for respiratory problems provoked by allergies. This treatment uses essential oils to penetrate the aroma in a room, using an oil burner or clay pot. Add between 5 to 8 drops of an essential oil and allow to evaporate. With this method do not use a vehicle or neutral oils, because they can overheat and give off an unpleasant aroma.

■ **Baths.** Very useful in relieving tensions and unpleasant symptoms brought on by allergies. Fill a bathtub with hot water and add a few drops of aromatherapy oil and soak in the water. It's advised that you keep the doors and windows closed, so that the aroma from the oil and steam don't escape the bathroom. For a home made bath oil, mix 3 tablespoons of a neutral oil such as sweet almond oil and 50 drops of essential oil or a blend of essentials. Keep in a colored glass bottle. Use 1 to 2 teaspoons to each bath. To add essential oils directly to a bath use 4 to 8 drops.

■ **Massages.** The chemical compounds of essential oils can be absorbed into the skin, then entering the blood stream to produce chemical reactions similar to some medications.

VAPORS

This may be the best way to treat respiratory problems related to allergies such as hay fever. Fill a glass or a large cup half full with water almost on the boil and add 3 drops of an essential oil. Cover your head with a towel, close your eyes and breath in the steam.

A RECIPE FOR EACH DISCOMFORT

Aromatherapy can be especially useful in treating skin allergies because aromatherapy is primarily a topical therapy. At the same time it's very effective for respiratory discomforts in the form of steam baths or vapor treatment. We've put together a practical guide with recipes to help relieve the discomforts brought on by a number of allergies.

For the respiratory system

If you want to relieve respiratory tract discomforts, use thyme essential oil added to vapor treatments or a hot bath.

Night time inhalation

Inhaling vapor with 2 or 3 drops of essential oil of eucalyptus, thyme, rosemary or mint added is very effective for asthma. It's recommended using this treatment before going to bed. During spring and summer, when you suffer from seasonal hay fever, we

When blending oils you shouldn't mix essential oils that have opposite therapeutic effect or use more than 3 or 4 oils at a time. A blend should be pleasant.

recommend placing an aromatherapy clay pot or vaporizer with essential oil in your bedroom.

Relieving congestion

To get rid of excess mucus caused by an allergic reaction, you can externally massage your nostrils and sinuses using essential oil of lavender, sweet thyme, hyssop, cypress, and eucalyptus blended with sweet almond oils. If you like, you can use the same essential oils for inhalations.

Balsamic cream

For slight eczema in a specific area or all over the body. It's best to use a non-fragrant free lotion or cream suited to sensitive skin. Use 1 teaspoon of cream or lotion with 2 drops of camomile and 2 drops of lavender. You can increase the amount of essential oils, up to 10 drops if the skin reacts favorably.

Back and chest massage

Mix 5 drops of essential oil of thyme and 5 drops of essential oil of eucalyptus with 2 teaspoons of olive or sunflower oil. Massage on the chest and back up to twice a day. While giving or receiving a massage, add 5-10 drops of oil to a clay pot for 30 minutes for vaporization.

SKIN ALLERGIES

Essential oils shouldn't be applied directly to the skin, especially if you have sensitive skin or are suffering from skin problems. Dilute in a neutral, or vehicle oil such as sunflower or almond oil. Use a proportion of 1 part essential oil to 20 parts neutral oil. For example: 5 drops of essential oil to 1 teaspoon of neutral oil. You can use a blend of geranium, clary sage and thyme gently applied to the affected area for a potentially beneficial relief.

Natural relief

There are a number of medicinal herbs that might be very beneficial for the prevention and relief of allergy symptoms. The following is a guide to many therapeutic plants, with simple recipes to be used every day. In addition, essential oils from A to Z, made with herbs, are for topical use and help in the treatment of allergies.

Fitotherapy is one of the oldest curing arts. Since ancient times cultures have used remedies extracted from natural plants, especially herbs and plants for internal use or external applications to cure the human body. This ancient folk knowledge about the curative powers of plants has been inherited today to relieve and treat a number of discomforts. The essential herbs and recipes included in the following pages are especially indicated to relieve allergy symptoms. They are natural and if used properly don't cause any harm, although it's advised before using them to consult your doctor to take advantage of the beneficial relieving powers of natural herbs.

Burdock
(Arctium majus)

- **Parts used.** The roots and leaves, to prepare in infusions or to make tinctures.
- Belongs to the cardos family, although it's native to Europe, it can be found in China and the United States.
- It is principally used as a blood purifier

> ### BURDOCK ROOT TINCTURE
>
> *For skin ailments, especially eczema caused by allergy, take 20 drops of the tincture diluted in water, 2 to 3 times per day for 4 weeks.*

because it eliminates toxins from the body. This plant is also used to treat conditions such as psoriasis, eczema and other skin problems. The root is used for headaches, cough and sore throats.

• **Warning.** This plant shouldn't be used during pregnancy.

Marigold
(Calendula officinalis)

• **Parts used.** Petals and flower tops are used to prepare infusions or to make ointments, creams and lotions.

• Native to Europe, this garden plant looks like a large yellow or orange colored daisy.

• It is very beneficial for the treatment of many skin problems such as acne, eczema and psoriasis, and in relieving other general skin inflammations.

AGAINST SKIN ERUPTIONS

Skin eruptions as a result of allergies, infections or irritated skin, you can apply an ointment, cream or lotion with marigold directly onto the part of the skin with eruptions or rash, 2 to 4 times a day.
For a lotion, prepare an infusion with 2 teaspoons of marigold flowers in 1 cup of water.
Drain, let cool and apply.

ESSENTIAL OILS FROM A TO Z

ANGELICA

Earthy, sweet and penetrating aroma. When applied over the skin it helps to relieve skin eruptions and skin affections. When inhaled this oil is useful to decongesting the nose. It also helps to relieve coughs, headaches and bronchitis. Combines with geranium, grapefruit, lemon and camomile.

EUCALYPTUS

Because of its decongestive properties this oil is very effective in fighting against respiratory problems. It helps treat headaches brought on by colds and hay fever. It has a clean, potent and refreshing aroma that rejuvenates the nervous system and gives off a stimulating sensation.
On the skin, it helps to cure a number of skin ailments, including herpes.

WARNING

Essential oils are for external use **only**, they should **never** be ingested. Keep stored away from children and keep away from your eyes.

Echinacea
(Echinacea spp)

- **Parts used.** The roots and rhizomes are used to prepare infusions or to make tinctures.
- Native to North America, today it is cultivated throughout the world.
- This plant has a number of active properties that act on the immune system. It tends to be used as a blood purifier, especially for skin problems, because it eliminates dermatological alterations such as skin eruptions, acne and eczema. Echinacea also facilitates the action of interferon, a natural chemical mediator which helps the body's healing response to viral infections such as colds and flu, herpes and hay fever.

English ivy
(Hedera helix)

- **Parts used.** The leaves and young stems.
- This vine plant with perennial leaves, is native to moist forests in Western, Central and Southern Europe. It shouldn't be confused with poison ivy (*Rhus toxicodendrum*), which is found in the Americas.
- English ivy has a high content of saponines that help to reduce mucus in the respiratory system, this plant acts as an expectorant. It has antispasmodic properties, especially for the bronchial tubes and is a constrictive, it fights against blood clots and is an antibiotic. When

INFLAMED BRONCHIOLES

Drink ¹/2 teaspoon of echinacea tincture, diluted in a glass of water, 2 or 3 times a day. 2 cloves of garlic a day can accompany this internal remedy.

used internally, it can be used for constant cough and respiratory conditions such as bronchitis and asthma. Used externally it is an analgesic and can be used to fight cellulitis, arthritis, headaches and ulcers.

• **Warning.** You should never eat the fruit from this plant, because it can cause vomiting and diarrhea. It is not recommended during pregnancy. This plant can irritate sensitive skin.

TO RELIEVE COUGH

Place 2 teaspoons of dried English ivy in 1 cup and add hot water. Let sit and steep for 3 minutes. Drain and drink 3 cups a day. You can add a little honey to sweeten. You can also make this infusion adding liquorice, using the proportion of 1 teaspoon of English ivy to 1 teaspoon of liquorice root.

ESSENTIAL OILS FROM A TO Z

GINGER

Its spicy, intense and warm aroma soothes pains brought on by humidity, this is why it helps to reduce nasal congestion, along with a calming and stimulating effect. Combines with atlas cedar, eucalyptus, myrrh, lemon, neroli, camomile, sandalwood and vetiver.

Safety. People with sensitive skin should use ginger diluted, when using it in massages and in baths.

LAVENDER

Ideal for fighting bronchial problems, hay fever, headaches, flu and asthma. It is also tends to be used to reduce blood pressure and prevent heart palpitations. It is an effective bug repellent, and can be used on insect bites, wounds and rashes. Blends with geranium, jasmine, lemon, camomile, rose, and pine.

Safety. Shouldn't be used during pregnancy.

Lapacho tree
(*Tabebuia avellanedae*)

• **Parts used.** The inner bark of the lapacho tree is used to prepare decoctions and to make tinctures.

• Native to Brazil and Argentina, it has extended to other parts of the American continent.

• It has a direct action on the immune system and helps to fight bacterial and viral infections, especially of the ear, nose and throat. Its detoxifying power helps in treating skin problems.

Mint
(*Menta piperita*)

• **Parts used.** The leaves are used to prepare infusions and to make essential oils.

• Native to Europe, this herb is widely used in the culinary world, and is cultivated throughout much of the world.

• Much recommended for relieving skin eruptions, because it helps the skin to recover faster. Applied externally it has a calming effect, helping the mind and body to relax. This oil has anti-bacterial properties. It relieves coughs, colds and the flu.

• **Warning.** This remedy is not recommended for children under the age of 12 (neither in infusions nor as a topical essential oil) or for

ANTIALLERGIC MINT

As a decoction, drink 1 cup 3 times a day. As a tincture, drink 60 drops 3 times a day.

NASAL CONGESTION
To relieve nasal congestion, add a pinch of mint to an infusion made with equal parts of yarrow and elderberry. This is an excellent remedy against excess mucus.

mothers who are breast-feeding, because this herb may affect breast milk production. It should be avoided if you feel weak or are suffering from prolonged fevers.

ESSENTIAL OILS FROM A TO Z

MARJORAM

Helps to relieve pressure caused by excess mucus in the chest and asthma, bronchitis and sinus infection symptoms. On the skin it improves blood circulation and comforts the skin. Combines with Atlas cedar, cypress, lavender, rosemary, palisander, ylang ylang.
Safety. When used excessively this oil can cause drowsiness. It's best to avoid using it during pregnancy and it shouldn't be used for small children.

MYRRH

This resistant and penetrating aroma with a touch of lemon, has a powerful effect on the mucous membranes, which is why it helps to decongest the lungs and respiratory system. One form of use is inhaling a few drops of myrrh on a tissue or handkerchief. Because of its calming effects, it's beneficial in stressful situations.
On the skin it has a double effect, tonic and restoring.

Evening primrose
(*Oenothera biennis*)

- **Parts used.** Stems, leaves and seeds.
- Native to Europe, this plant has many essential fatty acids that act as cell and inter-cell mediators. It has anti-inflammatory and antiallergenic properties.
- The high content of tannins found in the stems and leaves gives the herb its curative properties, useful for injuries and irritations. However, the plant's most important active ingredient is found in the oils extracted from the seeds that can effectively reduce the symptoms related to skin diseases.
- **Warning.** This plant shouldn't be used during the first three months of pregnancy or for people who suffer from epilepsy. The oil should be prepared by professionals and not at home.

PRECIOUS PEARLS
You can purchase primerose oil in pearls (soft-gels) of 500 mg strength. If you prefer not to swallow the capsule, you can break it and extract the oil to add to a liquid. It's recommended using for at least 8 weeks in order to see visible improvements in skin affections.

Violet
(Viola tricolor)

• **Parts used.** The aerial parts of the plants are used to make infusions.

• It is grown in Europe, North Africa and other temperate zones in Asia, and even on the American continent.

• This is an excellent purifying herb, recommended for relieving skin conditions such as eczema and allergic problems. The infusion is a great wash for skin eruptions. Because of its expectorant properties, it is used against bronchitis and compulsive cough.

INFUSION FOR SKIN ERUPTIONS
Prepare an infusion and apply directly on the skin as a compress or soak for 5 minutes.

ESSENTIAL OILS FROM A TO Z

ROMAN CAMOMILE

This oil is especially good for hypersensitive skin, which tends to have allergic reactions to different cosmetics. It is good for the treatment of a number of physical discomforts caused by stress, such as some skin conditions. Blends with angelica, clary sage, geranium, jasmine, lavender, neroli, rose, ylang ylang. **Safety.** This oil shouldn't be used in the first four months of pregnancy. In high doses it can have an hypnotic or sedative effect.

ROSEMARY

Has a strong, clean and refreshing aroma that is an effective decongestant in fighting respiratory infections and lung ailments. It also helps to revitalize and stimulate the central nervous system. It blends with Atlas cedar, myrrh, geranium, ginger, grapefruit and basil. **Safety.** Don't use during pregnancy or if you suffer from epileptic attacks or for high blood pressure.

TINCTURE FOR HAY FEVER

For cases of allergies, especially hay fever, tincture made with elderberry can be useful. Take 1 teaspoon 3 times a day.

Elderberry
(*Sambucus nigra*)

- **Parts used.** Flowers, leaves and bark are used to prepare infusions and make tinctures.
- This is a common tree in Europe.
- The flavonoids it contains, including quercetin, are believed to account for the therapeutic effects of the elderberry flowers and berries. Thanks to these acids this plant has anti-inflammatory properties. This plant is very good for the respiratory system in general, but particularly for specific allergic reactions such as seasonal hay fever. It also has diaphoretic effects that stimulate the elimination of toxins through sweat, which is very good for colds and flu.

Thyme
(*Thymus vulgaris*)

- **Parts used.** The entire plant is used in infusions or to make essential oils for topical use.
- Native to the Mediterranean. Today it's cultivated throughout the world.
- This plant is an effective remedy for the respiratory system. It has expectorant and antiseptic therapeutic effects, which is why it's ideal for fighting respiratory infections and

DECONGESTANT
Thyme flowers infusion can be used as a vapor inhaler to clean the nasal cavities.

other respiratory problems such as asthma, hay fever, sore throats and cough. Timol, one of the plant's therapeutic components, acts as an antispasmodic and also has sedative and antiviral effects.

• **Warning.** This plant shouldn't be used in excessive doses. Do not ingest the essential oil. This essential oil shouldn't be used topically during pregnancy.

FIGHTING COUGHS

Because thyme is an antiseptic for the entire respiratory system, it's recommended drinking an infusion 5 times a day. For a dry cough, it is recommended to blend it with liquorice root powder in equal parts and preparing it as an infusion. Drink 1/2 cup, 6 times a day. You can also mix equal parts of each tincture and take 1 teaspoon and drink up to 5 times a day, diluted in water.

ESSENTIAL OILS FROM A TO Z

SANDALWOOD

Stimulates the immune system, fights sore throat and respiratory infections. On the skin it has a regulating and anti-inflammatory effect on dry eczema. It helps to soothe rashes and scaling skin. At the same time it helps to reduce nervous tension and anxiety. Combines with bergamot, cypress, myrrh, geranium, jasmine, lavender, lemon, inciense, neroli, basil, vetiver and ylang ylang.

TEA TREE

Tea tree oil helps to strengthen the immune system. This oil may be an effective remedy against the flu and headache because of its repairing action over the respiratory system, contributing in the relief of asthma, as well as bronchitis and sinus infections. On skin, this oil can act as an antiseptic and cleaner. It helps to fight acne, herpes, insect bites and dandruff.

What causes food allergies?

In treating food allergies, the first step is finding out what foods you are allergic to, keeping in mind that many times they may be several. Food and allergic reactions vary from person to person. Next, you should find a nutritional substitute to make sure that you keep a balanced, healthy diet.

NOTE
You should always consult your doctor before changing your diet.

✚ A food allergy occurs when your immune system responds defensively to a specific food that is not harmful to most people. When you eat the offending food, your immune system responds by creating specific disease-fighting antibodies that release large amounts of histamine in an effort to expel the "foreign invader" from your body. Histamine is a powerful chemical that can affect the respiratory system, gastrointestinal tract, skin or cardiovascular system. Although vary rare, there are a number of food allergies that can cause death (such as asphyxia). The most common food allergies are in reaction to:

- wheat and wheat derived foods;
- dairy products;
- eggs;
- peanuts;
- shell fish;
- some types of fish;
- nuts and dried fruits;
- soy beans;
- yeast;
- chocolate.

HOW ARE FOOD ALLERGIES DIAGNOSED?

Knowing what food causes allergy is not simple, only a few people have allergies to just one food. Also, allergic reactions can vary and are not always immediate. There are a number of tests to diagnose allergens, they vary from specialist to specialist. It's important that you research the possible tests and find out from your specialist what tests are best for you.

First test

If you suspect that a certain food causes your allergic reaction, it's recommended to cut that food from your diet for 10 days, observing any changes in your body. If the symptoms diminishes or disappear, you will need to completely eliminate that food from your diet. If you don't notice any change or if your symptoms continue, it's important to consult an allergist or specialist to diagnose your allergy through precise tests.

UNLIKELY FOOD ALLERGIES

Rice, sunflower and olive oils, sweet potatoes, broccoli, cauliflower, rabbit, peaches, pears and carrots.

The most susceptible, children

Little ones, especially babies, are more susceptible than adults to food allergies. It's estimated that one in ten children suffer from an allergy, although eight out of ten children with this ailment tend to get over the problem before they are five years of age. Among the most frequent causes are formulas, derived from cow's milk, that substitute mother's breast milk. In addition, milk and eggs tend to be the cause of eczema in children. It's important that babies don't eat any foods containing gluten (most cereals) for the first six months, because they haven't developed the enzymes to digest this protein. The same goes for honey, which should be avoided for the first year of life.

DAIRY ALLERGIES

Dairy products can act as allergens, especially for small, breast-feeding children. A reaction can be so severe as to cause bronchial spasms and asthma attacks. This may be due to a type of protein found in milk that is difficult for little ones to break down and introduce into the body, because it contains a chemical structure designed for a calf, which weighs 287 lb/130 kg. When compared to a baby's size, 7 to 22 lb/3 to 10 kg, it's understandable why children easily suffer from allergies to cow's milk. In the case of an allergic reaction it may be convenient to avoid dairy products (pure milk as well as powdered milk or other formulas) and replace them with sesame, soy, coconut or almond milk. Studies have also shown that children may be less allergic to goat's milk.

Warning. Chicken eggs can also be allergenic.

FOR PROPER CALCIUM INTAKE

Eliminating milk and other dairy products from the diet can bring on a calcium deficiency. To avoid this, you can substitute daily, always consulting your physician before:

- **Soy or sesame milk.** 1 glass or cup (preferably organic). Almond milk is also recommended.
- **Wholegrain cereals.** 1 small bowl (2 oz/60 g uncooked)
- **Vegetables.** 2 full plates, if possible raw.
- **Fruit (seasonal fruit).** 3 portions.
- **Bread (wholewheat).** 4 slices.
- **Beans.** 1 tablespoon (or 1 full plate once a week).
- **Tofu (soy cheese).** 2 tablespoons.
- **Granola.** 1 cup, to substitute 2 slices of bread, if you're on a diet.
- **Soy.** Flour, beans or patties (in this case, twice a week).
- **Nuts.** 12 almonds or hazelnuts.
- **Sesame (whole).** 2 teaspoons.
- **Poppy seeds.** 1 teaspoon.
- **Brewer's yeast.** 2 tablespoons.

BE CAREFUL WITH LABELS

"Non-diary" on labels means that the product doesn't contain butter, cream or milk. However, this label doesn't necessarily mean that the food doesn't include other ingredients derived from milk. This is why it's important to carefully read all the ingredients on the label. Processed meats, including hot dogs and other deli meats tend to have milk and other dairy products added. Other foods that can contain milk:

- Foods with black sugar.
- Foods containing caramel.
- Chocolate.
- High-protein flour.
- Margarine.

Wheat allergies

Allergic reaction to wheat is an abnormal response in the body against the protein found in this food. There is an infinite number of products made with this grain, in order to identify and avoid wheat it's important to carefully read all food labels. People with wheat allergies should not eat any product that contains: bread crumbs, whole grains, cereal extract, couscous, salted crackers, wheat flour (especially high protein, enriched with gluten), wheat gluten, malt or wheat starch. Wheat can also be found in: starch gelatin, dehydrated vegetable protein, starches, and vegetable gums.

To substitute wheat in a number of recipes, keep in mind equivalents and portions.

1 cup of wheat flour is equivalent to:

- *1 cup of rye flour.*
- *1 cup of potato flour.*
- *$1^1/_3$ cups of oat flour.*
- *$^1/_2$ cup of potato flour + $^1/_2$ cup of rye flour.*
- *$^5/_8$ cup of potato starch.*
- *$^5/_8$ cup of rice flour + $^1/_3$ cup of rye flour.*

WHEAT FREE DIET

Breakfast and snack
Fruit or vegetable juice. Seeds. Rice cakes with cream cheese and/or honey. Or yogurt with sesame seeds or homemade crackers with oatmeal, honey and raisins.

Mid morning
Fruit (fresh or dried).

Lunch and dinner
Rice noodles or brown rice with vegetables.
Lean meat, skinless chicken, fish, accompanied by vegetables and 1 egg.
Lentils, beans, peas, chickpeas with vegetables.
Tart made with a homemade dough, made from rice and oat flour.
Fruit.

Gluten allergy

People who are allergic to gluten have trouble absorbing these nutrients because gluten proteins harm the small intestine's lining. This provokes an allergic reaction with symptoms of bloating, anaemia, diarrhea and weight loss.

Gluten is found in grains such as wheat, rye, barley and oat, which should be completely avoided. To keep a balanced diet you should eat plenty of:

- *Fresh fruit and vegetables.*
- *Gluten free cereals such as quinoa.*
- *Eggs, milk, cheese, meat, chicken and fish are also valid alternatives.*

Peanut allergies

Peanuts are very allergenic and can cause fatal reactions if ingested by people with allergies to certain proteins found in peanuts. You need to carefully read all food labels to make sure that the food doesn't contain any of the following ingredients.

- *Peanut oil.*
- *Ground nuts.*
- *Mixed nuts.*
- *Peanut butter.*
- *Peanut flour.*

You should also keep in mind that some ethnic foods and some industrially processed or cooked foods, candies or soft drinks can contain peanuts and derivatives.

Defenses get ready to act!

The most sure and simple treatment for getting over an allergy is avoiding the allergen itself, but also reinforcing your immune system with a healthy and balanced diet.

There are nutrients that are fundamental in keeping the immune system strong, a nutritional deficiency can weaken your body's natural defenses. Among these nutrients, foods with **vitamin A**, derived from animal products: **dairy products**, **butter** and **fish oil**; and from vegetable products: orange colored fruits and from vegetables (**carrots**, **squash**, **asparagus**, **melon**, **peaches**, **apricots**), red (**tomato**, **beets**) and deep green vegetables (**spinach**, **kale**, **radishes**, **lettuce**, **parsley**). These are also important foods for **vitamin C**, which is widely known for its effective action in preventing colds. Vitamin C also acts on the entire immune system, strengthening and preventing other infections. Vitamin C rich foods include: **guava**, **kiwi**, **mango**, **cherries**, **rosehips**, **pineapple**, **citrus fruit**, **melon**, **strawberries**, **berries**, **peppers**, **tomatoes** and leafy vegetables such as **broccoli**, **cabbage** and **cauliflower** and other garden fruits and vegetables.

EVERY DAY

For the body to get the necessary amount of vitamin C you should drink 1 glass of fresh squeezed orange juice daily. For juices, you should always drink fresh squeezed, if you leave them out or store them in the refrigerator they lose some of their nutrient properties.

TO PREVENT ASTHMA

Wash 1 cup of sesame seeds, dry them in the sun and toast them. Mash 1 cup of nuts with the sesame seeds and $1/2$ cup of ginger to extract the juice. Mix well all the ingredients and store in an airtight container.
Eat 3 to 5 teaspoons of this mixture, 2 to 3 times a day.

Another immune stimulating vitamin is **vitamin E**. Vitamin E rich foods include: **wheat germ oil**, **soy oil**, **cereal grains** or **wholewheat grains**, **olive oil** (extra virgin olive oil, uncooked), **green leafy vegetables** and **nuts**. Also, **sunflower seeds**, **sesame seeds** and **flaxseeds** and **dried fruits** can help to prevent skin problems.

Another nutrient which is important but rarely mentioned is **folic acid** (**vitamin B$_9$**). A deficiency of folic acid causes a decrease in the body's ability to fight antibodies and can cause vulnerability to conditions such as anaemia and intestinal parasites. It is found in **beans**, **dried fruits**, **cabbage**, **spinach**, **broccoli** and other **green vegetables**, **almonds**, **peanuts** and **yeast**.

CARROTS FOR YOUR SKIN
Eating 1 carrot daily as a snack is a good habit and helps to prevent many skin problems such as skin eruptions, eczema and dermatitis.

MINERALS ARE IMPORTANT TOO

Not only vitamins are important for your body's defenses; minerals also play a key role. Among them, **iron** is fundamental. Iron deficiency is quite common, especially in young people and in pregnant women. A lack of iron, reduces your body's immune defenses; this is why it's important to eat iron rich foods. They include: **red** and **white meats, beans, nuts, raisins, lentils, sunflower seeds** and some green vegetables (**artichokes, bitter greens, watercress** and **spinach**). It's also important to eat foods rich in **magnesium,** to keep the bronchial muscle clean and relaxed, improving breathing. This mineral is present in **nuts** (especially **almonds**), **soy, oatmeal, figs** and **dates**.

Manganese along with vitamins from the B group, provides the body with energy, while helping the body to metabolize nutrients. It strengthens the body's resistance to illnesses, fortifies the nervous system, stimulates breast milk production and reduces the risk of diabetes. Some manganese rich foods include: **whole grain cereals, nuts, rice** and **wheat, spinach, nuts, pineapple, common tea, cloves** and **ginger**.

You can't discount the importance of **zinc.** A deficiency of this mineral affects the immune system, especially the lymph organs and provokes a drop in the body's defenses. It's found in **shell fish, meat, brewer's yeast, wheat germ, oats, beans** and **nuts**.

WHAT YOU SHOULDN'T LACK IN YOUR DIET

Some foods (fried foods, saturated fats, coffee, sugar and alcohol) reduce your immune system's ability to fight off ailments. But there is a number of natural foods that increase your defenses:

• **Olive oil.** This oil contains a number of poli-unsaturated fats (oleic and linoleic acids), it stimulates the body's defense mechanism important for the heart and arteries.

• **Garlic.** Improves the potency of the T lymphocytes. Eating garlic helps the body to increase the number of its natural protective cells.

• **Fresh fruits and vegetables.** Because of their high content of vitamins, minerals and other nutrients, fresh fruit and vegetables play an important antioxidant and revitalizing role.

• **Yogurt.** Bacteria found in yogurt helps our immune system and strengthens the intestinal lining.

• **Seasonal fruits, onions, squash, carrots, pollen, honey, parsley, avocado, tomato,** and **fish** help to protect the body against allergies. It's recommended to eat fresh blue fish at least twice a week.

PROTECTING THE LIVER

Protecting the liver is important
for people with allergies. A good way
of protecting it is to avoid fried foods,
saturated fats and rich foods.
Lemon is also important. You can use
lemon as a condiment or in lemonade.

PROTECTING FOODS

Mediterranean diet

A Mediterranean diet is one of the most complete and widely recommended by nutritionists because of its ability to strengthen the body's defenses and to prevent the discomforts brought on by allergies. This is thanks to the diet's richness in nutrients, vitamins, antioxidants and the essential fatty acids found in olive oil and fish. Typical foods in this diet include:

■ **Olive oil**, widely used in Mediterranean cooking. It is rich in mono-unsaturated fatty acids. Many studies have shown that fatty acids regulate HDL ("good cholesterol") levels and LDL ("bad cholesterol") levels in the blood. This helps to prevent and protect the heart against cholesterol plaque building up in the arteries.

■ **Fish** has fats that are very beneficial for the health. Studies have shown that populations living on Greenland, whose diet is made up exclusively of fish, and no vegetable oils, have low incidences of heart disease. This is because of their high intake of the poli-unsaturated fats found in fish, more specifically Omega-3 fatty acids. This component increases HDL and lowers LDL.

■ **Beans, cereals** (rice, pastas and many other wholewheat foods), **fruits** and **vegetables** are plentiful in a Mediterranean diet. In addition to a wide variety, it contains vitamins, minerals, antioxidants, fiber and complex carbohydrates.

MISO, SPECIALLY DESIGNED FOR ALLERGIES

Miso is a savory paste made from fermented soybeans. It's helpful against the allergies produced when the body can't use the proteins in the intestines, and considers these substances invaders acting against them. Miso is high in healthy bacteria, generated during fermentation, that helps the intestines break down complex proteins. Animal protein fatigues the kidneys and leaves behind toxic residues that can harm the arteries, heart and nervous system; many times they can cause allergies and acid in the blood. Miso, helps to neutralize the effects of animal protein. Miso also contains **iron, calcium** and **phosphorus;** it's a great ingredient in soups and to put over boiled vegetables, cereals and beans.
Warning. Miso is high in salt and should be used in moderation, especially for cases of hypertension and kidney problems.

CUCUMBER SLICES WITH MISO DRESSING

Ingredients
- 1 tablespoon olive oil
- 1 small leek stalk or ¹/4 onion, thinly sliced
- 1 tablespoon miso
- 1 tablespoon shredded ginger root
- 1 mushroom (shitake) thinly sliced
- 1 large cucumber, sliced diagonally and finely.

Preparation
Heat in a wok or pot and cover with oil. Add all the ingredients, except for the cucumber and sauté over low heat, constantly moving for 4 minutes. Sit to cool and cover the cucumber slices with the dressing.

Soothing recipes

There are many recipes based on foods, including beverages and pastes for topical use, that help soothe some allergic processes.

To prevent asthma
• *Toast spinach seeds over low heat and grind. Eat 2 teaspoons of this powder or drink with lukewarm water, twice a day.*

Relief for asthma I
Ingredients. 2 cups tofu, 3 tablespoons malt and 2 tablespoons horseradish juice. Mix all the ingredients and filter. Drink this natural remedy, 3 times a day.

Relief for asthma II
Ingredients. 1 cup of sesame seeds, 1/2 cup fresh ginger, 1/2 cup candy sugar (mixture of sugars that give the consistancy of caramel) and 1/2 cup of honey.
• *Toast sesame seeds, extract juice from ginger and mix well with the sugar, and then add honey. Next, mix sesame seeds with the ginger juice. When it cools down, mix all the ingredients together and store in an airtight container. Eat 1 spoonful for dessert in the morning and at night.*

For allergic spots
Ingredients. 2 to 3 tablespoons of mulberry (fruit that comes from a shrub with the scientific name *Zizyphus jojoba*).
• Boil in water. Eat lukewarm or drink as a liquid 2 times a day, 1 in the morning and 1 at night, for a period of 4 weeks.

Against allergic dermatitis
Two recipes, one with cucumber the other with cabbage to relieve symptoms of allergic dermatitis.
• *Slice 1 or 2 fresh cucumbers and apply to the affected zone. You can also mash the cucumbers and apply them as a paste.*
• *Wash 1 cabbage, mash and apply as a paste to the affected area.*

Anti-inflammatory vinegar
For skin allergies, rashes and insect bites, apple cider vinegar is recommended by naturopathic practitioners for its anti-inflammatory, anti-allergenic and itch relieving properties.
• *Soak a cotton ball and apply on the affected area.*

Salad for damaged skin
The following salad, rich in vitamins A and E and poli-unsaturated fatty acids, is recommended as a natural treatment to repair the skin. For eczema, irritated skin, rashes or acne. Its recommended eating it daily.
Ingredients. 1 shredded carrot, spinach leaves, 1 fresh beet grated, orange slices and 2 nuts.
• *Dress with lemon, sea salt and extra virgin olive oil.*

COUGH RELIEVING HORSERADISH
For asthma and cough brought on by allergies, this recipe is very efficient:
• Ingredients. 2 cups of horseradish and an amount to taste of candy sugar (a mixture of sugars that gives the consistency of caramel).
• Finely chop horseradish, raw or cooked, until you extract the juice. Add sugar and eat.

index